GEO

ALLEN COUNTY PUBLIC LIBRARY

3 1833 04755 5351

FRIENDS OF ACPL

104

P9-EER-291

2.17

Lexile: _____

AR/BL: _____3.8_____

AR Points: _____0.5_____

MEDUSA

by Xavier Niz

Consultant:

Dr. Laurel Bowman
Department of Greek and Roman Studies
University of Victoria
Victoria, British Columbia

Capstone
press

Mankato, Minnesota

Capstone Press
151 Good Counsel Drive, P.O. Box 669, Mankato, Minnesota 56002
www.capstonepress.com

Copyright © 2005 by Capstone Press. All rights reserved.
No part of this publication may be reproduced in whole or in part, or stored in a retrieval
system, or transmitted in any form or by any means, electronic, mechanical, photocopying,
recording, or otherwise, without written permission of the publisher.
For information regarding permission, write to Capstone Press,
151 Good Counsel Drive, P.O. Box 669, Dept. R, Mankato, Minnesota 56002.
Printed in the United States of America

Library of Congress Cataloging-in-Publication Data
Niz, Xavier.
    Medusa / Xavier Niz; consultant, Laurel Bowman.
    p. cm.—(World mythology)
    Includes bibliographical references and index.
    ISBN 0-7368-2662-9 (hardcover)
    1. Medusa (Greek mythology)—Juvenile literature. [1. Medusa (Greek mythology)
2. Mythology, Greek.] I. Title. II. Series: World mythology (Mankato, Minn.)
BL820.M38N59 2005
398.2′0938′01—dc22   2003027204

Summary: Tells the story of Medusa, Perseus' quests to kill her, and describes the role of
myths in the modern world.

Editorial Credits
Blake A. Hoena, editor; Juliette Peters, series designer; Patrick Dentinger, book designer
    and illustrator; Alta Schaffer and Wanda Winch, photo researchers; Eric Kudalis,
    product planning editor

Photo Credits
Art Resource, NY/Giraudon, 18; Smithsonian American Art Museum, Washington, D.C., 4
Bridgeman Art Library/British Museum, London, UK, 14; Christie's Images, 8; Private
    Collection, 10; Southampton City Art Gallery, Hampshire, UK, 12; The Stapleton
    Collection, 16
CoasterGallery/Joel Rogers, 20
Corbis/Araldo de Luca, cover

1 2 3 4 5 6 09 08 07 06 05 04

TABLE OF CONTENTS

Medusa, painted by Alice Pike Barney, shows Medusa with snakes for hair.

MEDUSA

A popular story told by ancient Greeks and Romans was about a monster named Medusa (mih-DOO-suh). Medusa lived in faraway Okeanos. She was very ugly and had snakes for hair. Medusa also had a terrible power. Anyone who looked at her turned to stone.

Ancient Greeks and Romans believed that gods controlled their lives. Many stories said the gods punished people who made them angry. Medusa had not always been a monster. She once was a beautiful woman, but then she angered the goddess Athena (uh-THEE-nuh). Athena turned Medusa into a monster.

In stories, the gods helped heroes kill monsters. The Greek hero Perseus (PUR-see-uhss) was sent on a quest to kill Medusa. The gods Athena and Hermes (HUR-meez) gave Perseus gifts to help him. But Perseus still needed to find a way to kill Medusa without being turned to stone.

GREEK *and* ROMAN *Mythical Figures*

Greek Name: ATHENA
Roman Name: MINERVA
Goddess of wisdom and protector of heroes

Greek Name: ATLAS
Roman Name: ATLAS
Titan who held the heavens above the earth

Greek Name: DANAE
Roman Name: DANAE
Perseus' mother

Greek Name: GORGONS
Roman Name: GORGONS
Medusa and her sisters

Greek Name: HADES
Roman Name: PLUTO
Ruler of the Underworld

Greek Name: HERMES
Roman Name: MERCURY
Messenger of the gods

Greek Name: PERSEUS
Roman Name: PERSEUS
Hero who killed Medusa

Greek Name: POLYDECTES
Roman Name: POLYDECTES
King who sent Perseus on his quest to kill Medusa

Greek Name: POSEIDON
Roman Name: NEPTUNE
God of the sea

Greek Name: ZEUS
Roman Name: JUPITER
Ruler of the gods and Perseus' father

ABOUT MYTHS

Ancient Greeks and Romans told about Medusa and other monsters in stories called myths. People used myths to tell what they thought was right and wrong. Many myths were about heroes, such as Perseus. Heroes often performed difficult tasks. The ways in which heroes completed their tasks taught people how to face challenges in their own lives.

Myths also taught ancient Greeks and Romans to honor the gods. Gods helped heroes on their quests. But they helped only the people who honored them. The gods punished people who did not obey them.

Monsters played an important role in most myths. Heroes killed monsters to prove their strength and courage. The most famous Greek hero was Hercules (HUR-kyoo-leez). He killed many monsters. The Greek hero Theseus (THEE-see-uhss) killed the Minotaur (MIH-nuh-tor). The Minotaur was a half-bull, half-human monster. Perseus had to kill Medusa.

Dante Gabriel Rossetti painted *Aspecta Medusa*. This painting
shows Medusa before Athena turned her into a monster.

MEDUSA BECOMES A MONSTER

The monsters Keto (KEE-toh) and Phorcys (FOR-siss) were Medusa's parents. Medusa had monstrous sisters named Stheno (STHEE-noh) and Euryale (yoo-RYE-uh-lee). Stheno and Euryale could not be killed. They were immortal. Medusa was mortal, unlike her sisters. She could die. Medusa and her sisters were known as the Gorgons.

Medusa was very beautiful. Many men wanted to marry her. One day, the sea god Poseidon (poh-SYE-don) saw Medusa and fell in love with her. Medusa met Poseidon in one of Athena's temples. Medusa became pregnant with Poseidon's children.

Athena was angry that Poseidon and Medusa had met in her temple. Athena could not harm Poseidon. He was too strong. Instead, she punished Medusa. Athena changed Medusa into a monster. Medusa grew big tusks like a boar. Scales covered her skin. Medusa's hair changed into snakes. Medusa became so ugly that anyone who looked at her turned to stone.

Charles Kingsley painted *How Perseus and His Mother Came to Seriphos*. Perseus and Danae were pulled to shore after being caught in a fisher's net.

King Acrisius (a-KRISS-ee-uhss) ruled the city of Argos. He had locked up his daughter, Danae (DAN-ay-ee). He wanted to keep her from ever having children.

Danae's room had a window. Zeus (ZOOSS), the ruler of the gods, saw Danae through the window and fell in love with her. He visited Danae as a shower of gold light. Zeus and Danae had a son named Perseus.

Acrisius was angry with Danae. He put her and Perseus in a chest and tossed it into the sea. The chest washed ashore on Seriphos. King Polydectes (pawl-ih-DECK-teez) ruled this island.

Years later, Polydectes had a large dinner party. Each dinner guest had to bring the king a gift. But Perseus was too poor to buy a gift. Instead, he bragged that he would bring Polydectes Medusa's head. Polydectes accepted Perseus' challenge. The king hoped Medusa would kill Perseus. Then he could marry Danae. Perseus did not want his mother to marry Polydectes.

In *Perseus and the Sea Nymphs* by Edward Burne-Jones, the nymphs give Perseus gifts to help him on his quest.

The gods Athena and Hermes told Perseus that he must first find the Graiai (GRAY-ay). These three witches were sisters of the Gorgons. The Graiai could tell Perseus where to find Medusa.

The Graiai had only one eye between them. They passed the eye back and forth to allow each other to see. When Perseus found the Graiai, he stole their eye.

The Graiai begged Perseus to give them their eye back. Perseus said he would return the eye only if they helped him. The Graiai told Perseus where to find the Gorgons. They also told Perseus where to find the Nymphs of the North. These sea nymphs would give Perseus items he needed on his quest.

The Nymphs of the North gave Perseus several magic items. They gave him a pair of winged sandals, which he could use to fly. They gave him a magic bag. The bag grew to the size of any object that was put in it. They also gave him the helmet of Hades. Whoever wore this helmet became invisible.

This ancient Greek vase shows Medusa (center) after Perseus (left) cut off her head. Athena is on the right side of the vase.

THE DEATH OF MEDUSA

The gods Athena and Hermes gave Perseus items to help him kill Medusa. Hermes gave Perseus a strong sword. Athena gave him a bronze shield. Athena also told Perseus not to look directly at Medusa. If he did, he would be turned to stone.

Using the winged sandals, Perseus flew to Okeanos. There, he found the three Gorgons sleeping. Perseus quietly sneaked up on Medusa. He used his shield like a mirror to see where she was. He could look at Medusa's reflection in the shield without being turned to stone. Then with one swipe of his sword, Perseus cut off Medusa's head.

Medusa's sisters heard Perseus and woke up. Perseus put Medusa's head in the magic bag. He used the winged sandals to fly away.

The Gorgons had wings and flew after Perseus. Perseus put on the helmet of Hades. The helmet made Perseus invisible. The Gorgons could not see him, and Perseus escaped.

This etching, *Atlas Supports the Heavens on His Shoulders,* was created by Bernard Picart.

AFTER MEDUSA'S DEATH

Many strange things happened after Medusa died. At the time of her death, Medusa was pregnant with Poseidon's children. When Perseus cut Medusa's head off, her full-grown children leaped from her body. Chrysaor (KRIS-ay-or) was a powerful giant. Pegasus (PEG-uh-suhss) was a winged horse.

On his way home, Perseus flew over the deserts of northern Africa. Drops of blood fell from Medusa's head. The blood mixed with sand and turned into different kinds of snakes. Ancient Greeks used this story to explain why Africa's deserts are filled with snakes.

Perseus saw the Titan Atlas as he flew over Africa. Atlas was a giant who held the heavens above the earth. Perseus asked Atlas for food and shelter. Atlas refused and attacked Perseus. Instead of fighting, Perseus pulled Medusa's head from the magic bag. When Atlas saw Medusa's face, he turned to stone. Myths say that Atlas' body became the Atlas Mountains.

Jean Marc Nattier painted *Perseus, Assisted by Minerva, Presents the Head of Medusa to Phineus and His Companions*. Minerva is the Roman name for Athena.

Perseus had several adventures as he flew home. In Ethiopia, he saw Princess Andromeda (an-DRAH-muh-duh) chained to a rock. She was being sacrificed to a sea monster. Andromeda's parents told Perseus he could marry Andromeda if he saved her. Perseus fought the sea monster and killed it.

Andromeda had already promised to marry a man named Phineus (FIN-ee-uhss). Phineus and his soldiers attacked Perseus. Perseus saved himself by holding up Medusa's head. It turned the men to stone.

When Perseus returned home, King Polydectes was about to marry Danae. To stop the marriage, Perseus used Medusa's head to turn the king to stone.

After his adventures, Perseus gave Medusa's head to Athena. Some myths say that Athena buried it under the city of Athens. Ancient Greeks believed Medusa's head protected Athens from attacks.

People can ride the Medusa roller coaster at Six Flags Great Adventure in Jackson, New Jersey.

MYTHOLOGY TODAY

For ancient Greeks and Romans, the image of Medusa was a symbol of protection. People placed her image on armor and shields. They believed that it would scare away enemies and protect them in battle.

People still use Medusa's name and image. Scientists named a type of jellyfish after her. The medusa jellyfish is round with large tentacles sticking out from its body. People think the jellyfish looks like Medusa's head floating in the water.

One of the first floorless roller coasters is named Medusa. Riders travel through many twists and turns at about 60 miles (100 kilometers) an hour. The roller coaster is named Medusa because it scares almost everyone who rides it.

Today, people no longer believe that Greek and Roman myths are true. But people still enjoy them. Myths are exciting stories about heroes and monsters. Myths also teach people about the beliefs of ancient cultures.

Adriatic Sea

•Rome

ITALY

GREECE

•Troy

Aegean Sea

Ionian Sea

Athens

Argos•
Sparta•

SICILY

SERIPHOS

LEGEND

• City

Mount Olympus

CRETE

SCALE
Miles

0   100   200

0   100   200
Kilometers

Mediterranean Sea

GLOSSARY

ancient (AYN-shunt)—having lived a long time ago, or very old

culture (KUHL-chur)—a people's way of life, ideas, art, customs, and traditions

immortal (ih-MOR-tuhl)—able to live forever; immortal creatures, such as Stheno and Euryale, cannot be killed.

invisible (in-VIZ-uh-buhl)—not seen

mortal (MOR-tuhl)—not able to live forever; humans are mortal.

nymph (NIMF)—a female spirit or goddess found in a meadow, a forest, a mountain, a sea, or a stream

quest (KWEST)—a journey taken by a hero to perform a task

sacrifice (SAK-ruh-fisse)—to kill an animal or person in order to honor a god

temple (TEM-puhl)—a building used for worship

Titan (TYE-ten)—any one of the giants who ruled the world before the gods on Mount Olympus

READ MORE

Fanelli, Sara. *Mythological Monsters of Ancient Greece.* Cambridge, Mass.: Candlewick Press, 2002.

Hoena, B. A. *Athena.* World Mythology. Mankato, Minn.: Capstone Press, 2003.

Lattimore, Deborah Nourse. *Medusa.* New York: HarperCollins, 2000.

USEFUL ADDRESSES

**National Junior Classical
   League**
422 Wells Mill Drive
Miami University
Oxford, OH 45056

Ontario Classical Association
PO Box 19505
55 Bloor Street West
Toronto, ON M4W 3T9
Canada

INTERNET SITES

FactHound offers a safe, fun way to find Internet sites related to this book.
All of the sites on FactHound have been researched by our staff.

Here's how:
1. Visit *www.facthound.com*
2. Type in this special code **0736826629** for age-appropriate
   sites. Or enter a search word related to this book for a
   more general search.
3. Click on the **Fetch It** button.

FactHound will fetch the best sites for you!

INDEX